## CONTENTS

Introduction  4
Harriet Tubman  7
Elizabeth Cady Stanton  9
Woody Guthrie  11
Mohandas Gandhi  12
Irena Sendler  15
The Hollywood Ten  17
Claudette Colvin and Rosa Parks  18
Ruth Bader Ginsburg  21
The Greensboro Lunch Counter Sit-In  22
Martin Luther King Jr.  25
Larry Itliong, Dolores Huerta, and César Chávez  26
Richard Oakes and the Occupation of Alcatraz  28
The Tree-Sitters of Pureora  31
Father Luis Olivares and the Sanctuary Movement  32
Tank Man  34
Nelson Mandela  37
Ryan White  39
Ai Weiwei  40
"It Gets Better" Project  42
March for Our Lives  45
Greta Thunberg  46
Additional Information  48

# INTRODUCTION

*"Never doubt that a small group of thoughtful, committed citizens can change the world, indeed, it's the only thing that ever has."*—Margaret Mead

In 494 BCE, Rome was ruled by a small group of wealthy patricians, while the plebeians, or plebs, the huge majority of ordinary Romans, had no role in the government at all. Then one day the plebs simply put down their tools, shut their shops, and left the city. Without its soldiers, farmers, tailors, shopkeepers, carpenters, masons, millers, and bakers, Rome couldn't function. That is how, without resorting to war or revolution, the plebs of Rome changed an unfair system and won their rightful share of power.

Many centuries later, in 1846, a former schoolteacher, pencil-factory worker, and part-time handyman named Henry David Thoreau was thinking about nonviolent resistance, the same technique the plebs had used to fight injustice in Rome. Henry had used it himself once or twice. He'd worked on the Underground Railroad, secretly helping runaway slaves escape to freedom. And he'd gone to jail for refusing to pay taxes that supported a government that allowed slavery.

He believed that if a law was evil and obeying it would cause harm to others, it was his moral

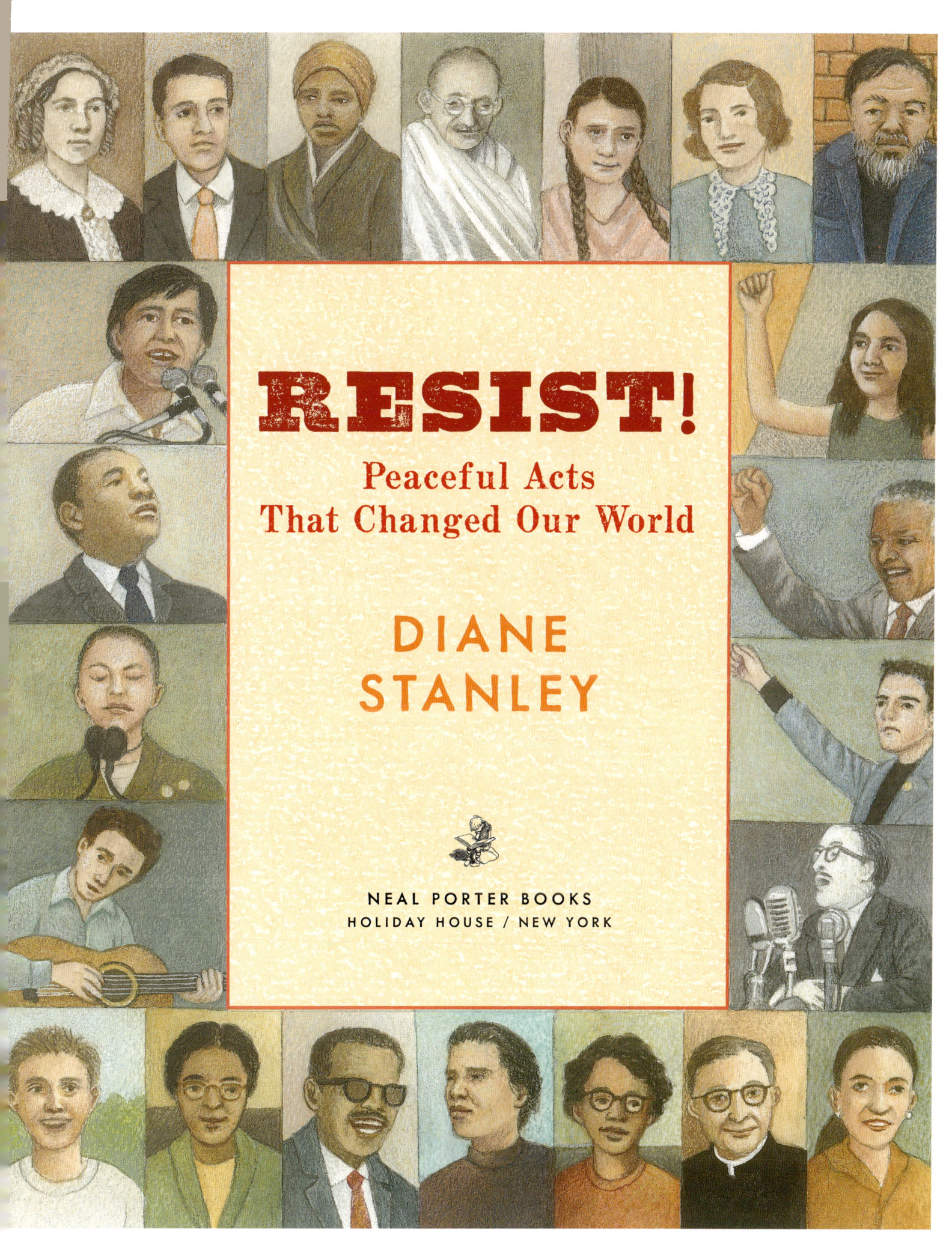

# RESIST!
## Peaceful Acts That Changed Our World

### DIANE STANLEY

NEAL PORTER BOOKS
HOLIDAY HOUSE / NEW YORK

*For Peter,*

*who has already made the world a better place*

Permission to use Jeff Widener's photograph of Tank Man
as the basis for an illustration courtesy of Associated Press.

Permission to reproduce a newspaper article about Ryan White
courtesy of the *Kokomo Tribune*.

Neal Porter Books
An imprint of Holiday House Publishing, Inc.

Text and illustrations copyright © 2020 by Diane Stanley
All Rights Reserved
HOLIDAY HOUSE is registered in the U.S. Patent and Trademark Office.
Printed and bound in January 2025 at Papercraft, Malaysia.
The artwork for this book was made using colored pencil
over a watercolor base on Arches cold-pressed watercolor paper.
Book design by Jennifer Browne
www.holidayhouse.com
First Paperback Edition, 2025
5  7  9  10  8  6

Library of Congress Cataloging-in-Publication Data

Names: Stanley, Diane, author.
Title: Resist! : peaceful acts that changed our world / Diane Stanley.
Description: New York City : Holiday House, [2020] | "Neal Porter Books."
Audience: Ages 7–10. | Audience: Grades 2–3. | Summary: "A non-fiction
look at how activists and artists throughout history have used peaceful
protests to change the world for the better"— Provided by publisher.
Identifiers: LCCN 2019038029 | ISBN 9780823444878 (hardcover)
Subjects: LCSH: Passive resistance—History—Juvenile literature.
Civil disobedience—History—Juvenile literature.
Protest movements—History—Juvenile literature.
Social change—History—Juvenile literature.
Classification: LCC HM1281 .S73 2020 | DDC 303.6/1—dc23
LC record available at https://lccn.loc.gov/2019038029

ISBN: 978-0-8234-4487-8 (hardcover)
ISBN: 978-0-8234-6076-2 (paperback)

EU Authorized Representative: HackettFlynn Ltd, 36 Cloch Choirneal,
Balrothery, Co. Dublin, K32 C942, Ireland. EU@walkerpublishinggroup.com

duty to peacefully resist it. And since Henry was a writer (along with all those other things), he wrote a groundbreaking essay on the subject, called "Civil Disobedience." Of course, Thoreau didn't invent the idea of peaceful resistance, but he literally wrote the book on it, taking an ancient idea and defining it for the modern age. Henry's little book would go on to inspire Mohandas Gandhi, Martin Luther King Jr., Nelson Mandela, and many, many others in their struggles for civil and human rights. They, in turn, would inspire others.

Nonviolent resistance can take many forms—from marching and carrying signs to sitting and refusing to move, making videos, writing books, singing songs, creating art, blogging, tweeting, filing lawsuits, and undermining oppressive regimes. It may take the form of a great movement led by a famous person. Other times it starts small and grows. Sometimes it's the quiet act of a single brave individual.

But whatever form it takes, nonviolent resistance is incredibly effective, because moral acts of courage are contagious. With the help of reporters and photographers who inform the public and spread the word, one brave act can stir countless others to join ongoing protests or start movements of their own. Because people throughout the ages have put themselves at risk for causes they believed in, tyrants have been overthrown, lives have been saved, and the world is a better and a fairer place. Here are just a few of their stories.

# HARRIET TUBMAN

*I Never Ran My Train Off the Track and I Never Lost a Passenger*

According to the law, Minty was the property of a white man. He'd bought her for cash, same as he'd buy an axe or a pair of Sunday shoes, so he could do with her as he pleased. He could beat her, work her to the bone, rent her out to his neighbors, or sell her to somebody else.

Minty couldn't respect a law like that. A person was a person, not a thing to be owned.

Her mother didn't respect it either. When their master tried to sell Minty's little brother to a man from Georgia, her mother met them at the door. "The first man that comes into my house," she said, "I will split his head open." Their master could have killed her for that, and the law would have allowed it. Amazingly, he backed away and the sale fell through.

Minty was so proud of her mother that when she grew up she adopted her name. So it was as Harriet, not Minty, that in 1849 she ran away from the man who owned her and headed north to freedom. She later recalled that when she crossed the border into Pennsylvania, she looked down at her hands to see if she was still the same person. "There was such a glory over everything; the sun came like gold through the trees, and over the fields, and I felt like I was in heaven."

Harriet could have stayed in Philadelphia, enjoying her new life as a free woman. But she couldn't help thinking about her family and friends. It felt wrong to be free when they were still enslaved. So she decided to go back and bring them out. She knew the way now, knew to hide by day and travel at night, following the stars. She was familiar with the forests and marshes, had learned which houses were "stations" on the Underground Railroad, knew where they could find shelter and food. So she walked back to Maryland the way she had come, a journey of ninety miles in the chill of December, knowing full well that if she was caught she would lose her freedom. Maybe even her life.

Yet she kept going back, time after time, making thirteen trips over the next eight years and guiding at least seventy slaves out of bondage. None of them were ever caught. People started calling her "Moses" because she'd led so many souls to the "promised land."

When slavery was finally abolished in 1865, Harriet didn't stop fighting injustice. She started working with Elizabeth Cady Stanton and Susan B. Anthony for the cause of women's suffrage. Because a person was a person, be they black or white, male or female. They all deserved the same rights to life, liberty, and the pursuit of happiness.

# ELIZABETH CADY STANTON

## *...That All Men and Women are Created Equal*

Elizabeth Cady was eleven when her older brother died. She would always remember trying to comfort her father by promising to model her life after her late brother. He'd turned to her and said, "Oh, my daughter—I wish you were a boy!" That was the moment she understood that however hard she worked to please him, she would always be a disappointment.

And it wasn't just her father. The whole world seemed to think that women were lesser beings. So wherever she turned, doors would be closed to her. She graduated at the top of her class but could not be admitted to a college as her brothers had. She spent countless hours mastering her father's law books but could never be a lawyer. And when she and her new husband, Henry Stanton, went to London on their honeymoon for the World Anti-Slavery Convention, the women, even elected delegates like Lucretia Mott, were not allowed to participate.

Elizabeth felt it was time things started to change. So in 1848 she, Lucretia, and a small group of friends got together to plan a convention of their own, the first ever held to advance the rights of women. For this "second revolution," Elizabeth wrote a Declaration of Sentiments. It began with a slight improvement on the Declaration of Independence: "We hold these truths to be self-evident: that all men *and women* are created equal."

Three hundred people came to the Seneca Falls, New York, convention, and at first it seemed a great success. Everyone was excited, everyone was in agreement, and every resolution passed with unanimous consent. Then Elizabeth read the resolution demanding votes for women. Cries of outrage filled the room. The idea was even too shocking for Lucretia. The resolution barely passed, and only because Frederick Douglass, the famous abolitionist, spoke in favor of it. But at least the revolution had begun. Now came the long, hard slog.

Elizabeth would spend the rest of her life working with Susan B. Anthony for the cause of women's rights—Elizabeth writing fiery speeches (or "forging thunderbolts," as Susan put it), while Susan traveled the country "firing them off."

American women didn't gain the right to vote until August 18, 1920. Elizabeth wouldn't live to see that day. But she had struck the flame that lit the torches that have been passed forward ever since, through generations of women and men who wanted nothing less than to free the *other* half of the human population.

# WOODY GUTHRIE

## *Hard Times*

Woody knew about hard times. He'd been on his own since the age of fifteen, bunking down with friends when school was in session and living the hobo life in the summers. He earned money by cleaning spittoons, picking up trash, shining shoes, or playing his guitar in saloons.

He'd watched as his hometown of Okemah, Oklahoma, went from oil boom to oil bust in a matter of years. He'd watched the farmers struggle through years of drought and dust storms. Watched everybody struggle through the Great Depression. And then, in April 1935, he'd watched as a towering black cloud came roaring across the plains like God's judgment at the end of the world. It buried houses and cars and carried off three hundred million tons of topsoil, leaving behind a wasteland known as the "dust bowl."

So Woody joined the great migration of "Okies" heading west on Route 66, their few belongings tied to their rattletrap jalopies. But in California they just found a different kind of misery—desperate families living in squalid migrant camps, picking cotton for starvation wages if they could find any work at all. Those images would haunt him for the rest of his life.

Woody wrote about the things he'd seen in a wonderful, homespun kind of poetry, then turned those poems into songs like "Hard Travelin'" and "Goin' Down the Road Feeling Bad." He wrote about migrant workers, farmers, miners, steelworkers, hoboes, breadlines—and those politicians who didn't seem to care. Through his songs, played on records and radio stations all over the country, Woody became the public voice of the poor and dispossessed. You didn't know about the hard times? Had missed them somehow? He'd sure paint you a picture!

His most famous song, "This Land Is Your Land," starts out as a feel-good love song to his country, with its golden valleys, diamond deserts, and wheat fields waving. Then, in the fourth stanza, the dust clouds roll in, the skies grow dark, and lines of hungry and hopeless Americans stand waiting for help from the government—clothes, food, maybe even a job.

Woody's songs of social protest touched the people who heard them, making them see and feel the suffering around them, making them care enough to do something about it. Even after his death, his songs led other musicians like Pete Seeger, Bob Dylan, and Bruce Springsteen to continue his work of bearing witness to injustice through the power of words and music.

# MOHANDAS GANDHI

## *A Little Walk with Friends*

On the morning of March 12, 1930, Mohandas Gandhi went for a walk. He was sixty but looked older, with a small, frail body, bald head, and little round spectacles. And though he was an educated man who had studied law in London, he dressed like an Indian peasant in a homespun dhoti and shawl. He wore sandals and carried a walking stick.

A group of friends had agreed to join him. Their destination, the coastal village of Dandi, was 240 miles away. It would take them twenty-four days to get there. When they arrived, they would go to the ocean and make salt by boiling seawater, as Indians had been doing for centuries. And this plan of theirs wasn't just unusual—it was dangerous.

Gandhi, of course, was no ordinary man. He was the leader of the Indian National Congress, and revered by the people of India. They called him *Mahatma*, or "great soul." They called him *Bapu*, meaning "father." And his walk to the sea would be the turning point in a long campaign of nonviolent resistance to British colonial rule.

It was illegal for Indians to make or gather salt (they had to buy it from the British and pay a tax). And any form of resistance, however peaceful, was a crime. So Gandhi and his friends would be breaking the law. They'd almost certainly be arrested and sent to prison. But that was the whole point of their protest: openly opposing the unjust laws of an oppressive government.

They were not alone in their courage. In every village they passed, people poured out of their homes to join the march. With each succeeding day, their numbers grew until they reached into the tens of thousands. Soon reporters and photographers arrived to cover the story. Newsreel cameras caught it all on film: British soldiers beating peaceful protesters; Gandhi leaning down to gather a crust of salt from the beach; the arrest of Gandhi and more than sixty thousand of his followers. Those images drew international support for Gandhi and independence.

The years that followed must have felt like treading water. The British hosted three conferences to discuss the India question, but nothing ever changed. Civil disobedience continued. Gandhi and his supporters were arrested again and again. It was not until after World War II, with Britain exhausted and financially strained, that the empire began to crumble. Finally, on August 15, 1947—seventeen years after Gandhi's March to the Sea—India gained its independence.

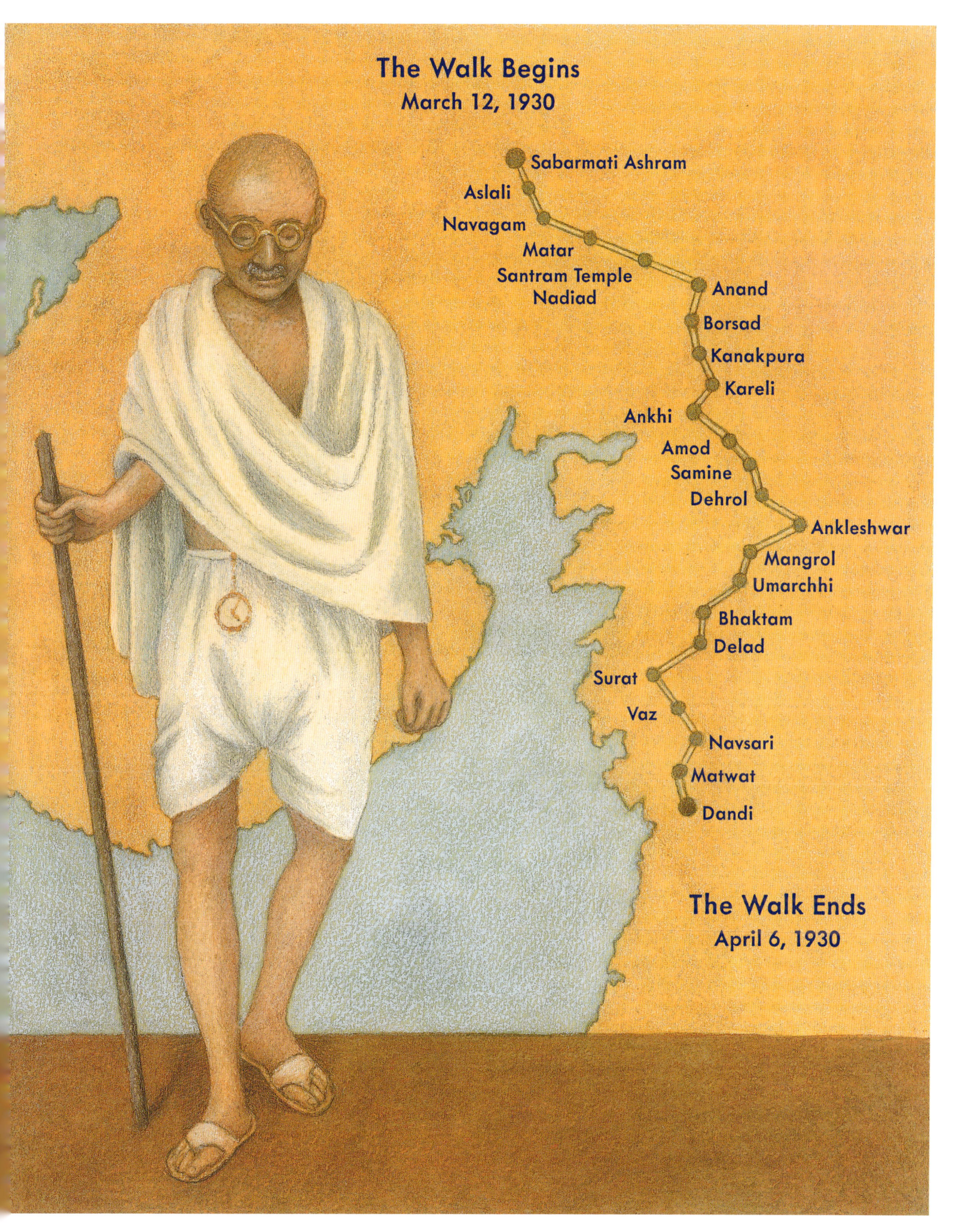

# IRENA SENDLER

## *If a Man Is Drowning, One Must Help Him*

Irena was living in Warsaw when the Germans marched into Poland. She'd heard what had happened to the Jews in other countries invaded by the Nazis. So she and her friends started forging documents so Jewish families could go into hiding under false Christian names.

Then the Warsaw Ghetto was established. It had been a Jewish neighborhood. Now the Germans turned it into a prison, surrounded by a ten-foot wall topped with barbed wire. Almost half a million Jews were forced to live there, crammed six or seven to a room, without nearly enough food or medical supplies.

As luck would have it, Irena was a social worker assigned to visit the ghetto to check the inmates for contagious diseases. This gave her perfect cover for bringing in desperately needed food and supplies. But it soon became obvious that she could never bring enough for all the prisoners. Despite her efforts, thousands were dying every month of sickness or starvation.

Irena remembered how her father, a doctor, had treated his poorest patients for free. He did this, he explained, because "If a man is drowning, one must help him." Irena saw the suffering in the ghetto as exactly that kind of emergency. *Everyone* there was "drowning." And since she couldn't possibly save them all, she determined to rescue the children.

For the next eighteen months, Irena and her helpers went to the ghetto every day, and they never left without at least one child. The older children were sneaked out through a church that backed onto the ghetto. They'd enter through a back door, remove their Star of David armbands, then exit along with the crowds of worshipers when the service was over.

The babies were carried past the checkpoints in whatever way she could devise: in packages or suitcases, garbage wagons or gunny sacks, handbags, coffins, even a mechanic's toolbox. But ambulances were the best. With the help of a sympathetic driver and a trained dog, she could get even the fussiest baby through. At the first sign of a whimper, she would tap the dog's paw and he would bark on cue, setting off the Nazis' dogs and drowning out the baby's cries.

Once outside the ghetto, the children were given new identity papers and taken into private homes, orphanages, and convents. Helping Jews was a crime punishable by death, yet no one ever refused to take a child from Irena. By the end of the war, she had saved 2,500 Jews, more than any other individual during the Holocaust.

# THE HOLLYWOOD TEN

## *But I'd Hate Myself in the Morning*

In October of 1947, a group of Hollywood directors, actors, producers, and scriptwriters were called to appear before Congress to answer the following question: Are you now, or have you ever been, a member of the Communist Party? For many of them, the answer would be yes.

During the Great Depression, the Communist Party was popular with idealistic people. It opposed fascist leaders like Hitler in Europe and fought for social justice at home. It was also perfectly legal. But after World War II, a Cold War developed between the U.S. and the communist Soviet Union. In the climate of fear and suspicion that followed, party members were branded as traitors or spies.

In the House of Representatives, the Un-American Activities Committee began collecting names and issuing subpoenas, often with no evidence, to persons who were "said to be" communists. If they admitted to having belonged to the party, they'd be "blacklisted"—fired from their jobs with little hope of ever finding another. If they'd been members but denied it, they'd be guilty of lying under oath. And if they simply refused to answer, they'd be charged with contempt of Congress. The only way out of this terrible dilemma was to give the names of fellow communists—saving themselves by destroying the lives of others.

A small group of men, known as the Hollywood Ten, chose not to answer on the grounds of their First Amendment rights. They knew it would cost them dearly. They'd be blacklisted, fined, *and* sent to prison. They'd lose their homes and their careers. But it was still better than submitting to injustice. As one of the ten, the Oscar-winning screenwriter Ring Lardner Jr. said, "I *could* answer the question . . . but if I did, I would hate myself in the morning."

Following their release from prison, some of the ten moved to Mexico or England. Most of the writers continued to work for minimal pay under false names. Then, slowly, the ice began to thaw. CBS started quietly hiring blacklisted artists. In 1960, the director Otto Preminger announced that his big new movie, *Exodus*, had been written by Dalton Trumbo, one of the Hollywood Ten. Six months later, at the insistence of the actor Kirk Douglas, Trumbo was given credit for a second important film, *Spartacus*. The blacklist was gradually coming to an end.

In time, the writers were given credit for their anonymous work (and the Academy Awards they'd been unable to accept). They'd paid a high price for taking a stand, but at last it was over. And they'd never had to hate themselves in the morning.

# CLAUDETTE COLVIN AND ROSA PARKS

*Standing Up by Sitting Down*

Claudette Colvin was an ordinary fifteen-year-old girl riding the bus home from school. She came from a poor African American family with very little education, but Claudette worked hard and made good grades. She had dreams for her future. She believed in herself. So when the bus driver ordered her to give up her seat to a white woman, something inside her snapped.

She said it "felt like Sojourner Truth was pushing down on one shoulder and Harriet Tubman was pushing down on the other, saying '*Sit down, girl!*'" So that's what she did. It was a daring thing to do in Montgomery, Alabama, in 1955. Claudette was arrested and found guilty of breaking the segregation laws. Her minister bailed her out of jail.

Nine months later, a well-dressed middle-aged woman named Rosa Parks also climbed onto a bus. She paid her fare, walked past rows of empty seats reserved for whites, and sat down in the "colored" section. But it was rush hour and pretty soon the bus was full. So the driver told the four passengers in the front row of the colored section to give up their seats and stand in the back so a single white man could sit there. Three of them did as they were told.

But Rosa was tired—and not just because she'd been on her feet all day. She was tired of being treated badly because of the color of her skin. Tired of the assaults on her dignity. Tired of giving in. So, like Claudette before her, she refused to budge and was arrested.

But that's not the end of either story. Rosa was a highly respected member of her community and the arrest deserved a response. So, under the leadership of a new young minister, Dr. Martin Luther King Jr., they planned a protest that would be peaceful, legal, and highly effective: they would simply stop riding the buses. It would mean hours of walking to work or to school, then more hours of walking to get home, but everyone agreed to do it. Before long, sympathetic whites had joined the protest. And all over the country, people read the news and cheered them on. So it continued—through the cold, and the rain, and the muggy heat of summer, while city buses sat idle and the transit company's finances tanked—for 381 days.

Meanwhile, as the first person arrested in Montgomery for refusing to give up her seat on a bus, Claudette had become a plaintiff in a federal lawsuit that went all the way to the U.S. Supreme Court. Almost two years after her arrest, segregation on public buses was ruled unconstitutional and the boycott came to an end. But the civil rights movement had just begun.

# RUTH BADER GINSBURG

## *Planting Seeds*

Only nine women, in a class of five hundred, were admitted to Harvard Law School in 1956. One of them was Ruth Bader Ginsburg. Shortly after she arrived, the dean invited the women to dinner. When the meal was over, he went around the table asking each of them how she justified taking a place that could have gone to a man. It was fair warning of what lay ahead.

Ruth hardly needed to justify her presence. She was a brilliant student and she worked hard, becoming the first woman ever elected to the *Harvard Law Review* and graduating at the head of her class. She did this while caring for a toddler and nursing her husband through a bout of cancer. Yet when she was recommended for a clerkship with a Supreme Court justice, he turned her down. So did all twelve law firms to which she applied—not because she wasn't qualified, but because she was a woman.

If the law treated half the population as second-class citizens, Ruth believed the law ought to be changed. So she began working with the American Civil Liberties Union to start a Women's Rights Project. A new wave of feminist leaders were already protesting, writing books, publishing magazines, and forming organizations for women's equality. But Ruth took a different tack: slowly, strategically, case by case, she chipped away at unjust laws.

She worked so hard and stayed so late that her husband, Marty, often had to go down to the office and make her come home to eat and get some sleep. He claimed, years later, that his life's greatest accomplishment was making it possible for Ruth to do what she did.

During her years at the Women's Rights Project, Ruth argued six carefully chosen cases before the Supreme Court, winning all but one. Some of them were surprising to people who didn't understand her strategy. Like the case of a widower whose late wife had been the family's primary wage-earner, yet he was denied Social Security benefits after she died—because only women could receive survivor's benefits. Or the case that overturned a Missouri law requiring men to serve on juries but making it optional for women. Ruth's goal was as simple as it was profound: that all persons, male or female, should be equal under the law.

Eighteen years later, in 1993, Ruth Bader Ginsburg became the second woman to serve on the Supreme Court, where she continued planting seeds for equality and justice, one case at a time.

# THE GREENSBORO LUNCH COUNTER SIT-IN

## *Not Really There for the Coffee*

On February 1, 1960, four college freshmen entered a Woolworth store in Greensboro, North Carolina. They bought a few things in the store, then stopped at the lunch counter. There weren't four seats together, so they split up and sat where they could. Then they ordered coffee.

"We can't serve you," the waitress said. The students were black and the counter was reserved for whites. But they weren't really there for the coffee. They had come seeking justice.

In the spirit of Gandhi's nonviolent protests, they waited patiently. They didn't react when people shot them dirty looks or when the manager told them to leave. Not even when a policeman started pacing back and forth behind them, slapping the end of his nightstick against his palm in a threatening manner. They just sat quietly and read or did their homework.

The whites at the lunch counter leaned away and gave them dirty looks. One sweet-looking elderly woman kept staring at them. Then, when she'd finished her doughnut and coffee, she came over and stood behind two of the students. "Boys," she said, "I am so proud of you. I only regret that you didn't do this ten years ago." It was a good moment.

The next morning, twenty-nine students came. And with each succeeding day the protest grew, till they numbered in the hundreds. The "sit-in" became a national news story, with TV coverage playing out in living rooms across the country. People were appalled by the angry mobs who poured soda and sugar over the heads of unresisting students, spat on them, and squirted them with ketchup. They were shocked to see peaceful students dragged off to jail.

Those images sparked new protests in cities all over the South—"wade-ins" at segregated beaches and pools, "pray-ins" at all-white churches, and "read-ins" at whites-only libraries.

Public support for desegregation was growing, yet Woolworth refused to budge. So the students decided to boycott stores with segregated lunch counters. Soon, with the city's African American community taking its business elsewhere, sales began to drop. The bad press was harming the Woolworth brand, its stores were losing a shocking amount of money, and there was only one way to make it stop. So on July 25, almost six months after the "Greensboro Four" had started their peaceful sit-in, Woolworth desegregated its lunch counter.

Today, a section of the lunch counter is on display at the National Museum of American History in Washington, D.C., and the former Woolworth in Greensboro is a civil rights museum.

# MARTIN LUTHER KING JR.

## *"Bombingham" and the Children's Crusade*

In 1963, Birmingham, Alabama, was the most segregated city in the United States. Nearly half of its residents were black, but the only work they could get was manual labor. African Americans weren't allowed to enter public parks, libraries, swimming pools, or golf courses. There were so many racially targeted bombings in the city, people started calling it "Bombingham." Dr. Martin Luther King Jr. and his team at the Southern Christian Leadership Conference hoped to change that situation.

Their campaign began with sit-ins and boycotts, then moved on to peaceful marches. Since few adults could afford to skip work to attend the marches, they recruited and trained almost a thousand children, from college age down to elementary schoolers. In what came to be called the "Children's Crusade," the young people marched in groups of fifty, through the downtown business district in the direction of City Hall, laughing, clapping, and singing freedom songs.

Enter the villain: Commissioner of Public Safety Eugene "Bull" Connor was a notorious racist, fully prepared to meet the "threat" of singing children with violence. First he turned fire hoses on them, the full force of the water knocking them down, flinging them over cars, and rolling them along the streets. Then he sent police dogs in to attack them. By the end of the day, 1,200 demonstrators were in jail. The youngest was nine years old.

The press recorded the whole disgusting episode. The Birmingham campaign became front-page news in America and beyond. Bull Connor's racist rantings and violent tactics were so grotesque that no one, as President Kennedy put it, could "prudently ignore them." Kennedy called for a Civil Rights Act, Connor lost his job, and two months after the campaign began, WHITES ONLY signs were coming down all over the city. African Americans were allowed to eat at lunch counters, use libraries, and enjoy public parks. It was a major turning point for civil rights.

It was a hard-won battle, one of many that King would face in a lifetime of struggle for racial justice. But he never let the Bull Connors of the world discourage him, because his faith in mankind was too strong. He held a dream in his heart of a future time in which people were judged for their character, not the color of their skin, and children of all races would join hands as sisters and brothers. King held that dream till his dying breath. Now it's up to us to carry it forward into a hopeful future.

# LARRY ITLIONG, DOLORES HUERTA, AND CÉSAR CHÁVEZ

### *¡Sí, Se Puede!*

The migrant farm workers of California were among the poorest and most desperate in the country. Laws that protected other workers did not apply to them. They labored in the fields from dawn to dusk, often without a break, for as little as $5 an hour. Often they had no access to clean water, bathrooms, or medical care. At night they slept in shacks, sometimes on the floors. And since the harvests were seasonal, they were always on the move, picking peas and lettuce when the weather was cold, then moving to another farm for cherries and beans, then corn and grapes, winding up with cotton in the fall. With no permanent home, their children couldn't go to school and break the cycle of poverty. They just worked in the fields with their parents.

Larry Itliong, a labor organizer, had been helping Filipino American farm workers for thirty-five years. In September of 1965, as the grape harvest was just beginning, his union voted to stop working till they were paid a living wage. Then Larry met with César Chávez and Dolores Huerta, labor organizers whose union members were mostly Latino. Would their workers be willing to join the Filipinos' strike? If they all stood together, the growers might be forced to make concessions. *Someone* had to pick those grapes or they'd rot in the fields!

The Latino workers knew what voting yes would mean for them. Without jobs to bring in money, they would lose what little savings they had. Yet they agreed to join their Filipino brothers and sisters. It was the only way that things would ever change. César insisted that the two groups always work together, and that they never resort to violence. Dolores came up with a motto for their first joint effort: *¡Sí, se puede! Yes, it can be done!*

In December they announced a boycott of grapes from nonunion farms. Inspired by Gandhi's March to the Sea, César organized a three-hundred-mile walk from the grape fields of Delano to Sacramento to raise awareness of their cause. Then he went to work convincing the public that the lives of more than two million workers could be changed for the better by something as easy as giving up grapes. He was a famously charismatic speaker and very persuasive. Soon, families all over the country proudly stopped buying grapes because it was the right thing to do.

Finally, after five years of hardship, the growers agreed to sign their first union contracts, giving their workers reasonable pay and appropriate benefits.

*¡Sí, se hizo! Yes, it was done!*

# RICHARD OAKES AND THE OCCUPATION OF ALCATRAZ

## *Taking Back the Rock*

Alcatraz, a rocky island in San Francisco Bay, had once been the site of a federal penitentiary, housing notorious gangsters like Al Capone and George "Machine Gun" Kelly. But the prison had been closed in 1963. Now it was just an uninhabited rock with a lot of old buildings on it.

Across the bay in San Francisco, Mohawk activist Richard Oakes saw an opportunity: according to the 1868 Treaty of Fort Laramie, the U.S. was bound to return any abandoned or out-of-use federal lands to the Indians who'd formerly owned them. Alcatraz fit that description perfectly. So in November of 1969, Richard and his fellow activists claimed the island for Indians of all tribes "by right of discovery" (since their ancient ancestors had discovered it more than ten thousand years before Columbus even showed up). Then eighty-nine Native activists sailed out to Alcatraz and settled in to stay.

Their dream was to build an Indian mecca there, a place where all indigenous people were welcome. It would have a federally funded university where Native American history and culture would be taught. There would be a museum, a cultural center, and a restaurant.

But the government refused all their demands, and life on the island was hard. The buildings had never been designed for comfort. Now they were crumbling. There was no heat, and only three working toilets. Food had to be brought over from the mainland. And as more protesters came—at one point there were four hundred—it grew crowded. Then the government shut off their electricity and phone service.

Nineteen months later, with only fifteen occupiers still on the island, armed marshals arrived to forcibly remove them. And rather than abiding by the Fort Laramie treaty, Congress designated Alcatraz Island a national park.

And yet the protest was a success. Because it was so widely covered by the media, the public learned about the ongoing loss of Native lands, rights, and cultural identity. As a result, government policies became more sensitive to indigenous needs and values.

As Richard Oakes famously said, "Alcatraz is not an island, it's an idea"—that Native Americans could recapture and control their own destinies. It was an idea that sparked a new wave of Native protests—from the Trail of Broken Treaties to the Longest Walk to Standing Rock—that continue to this day.

# THE TREE-SITTERS OF PUREORA

## *Little Houses in the Podocarp Trees*

New Zealand's North Island was once wild and green, with vast stretches of ancient old-growth forest. Then European settlers arrived. They chopped down the oldest and tallest trees for wood to build their houses. The smaller trees and undergrowth they burned, clearing the land for farming and sheep grazing. Little by little, the ancient woodlands disappeared.

One of the few that remained was the lush and mountainous Pureora rain forest, where towering podocarp trees had been standing for more than a thousand years. Soft green moss and thickets of tree ferns grew along the banks of clear, rushing streams. Birds fluttered through the canopy. Rare wildlife found safety in the undergrowth. Then, in 1978, loggers came to Pureora with bulldozers and chain saws to cut the forest down.

Enter Stephen King—not the famous author, but a soft-spoken, long-haired, frequently barefoot young man from Auckland, who was not about to let that happen. So he and several like-minded friends drove down to Pureora, got a legal camping permit, and proceeded to set up camp—not on the ground, but in the trees.

Using thick, woody vines as ropes, they climbed the trunks of the trees and perched in the high branches. With people now occupying the forest, the loggers had to stop work. But they didn't go away. They planned to wait the protesters out.

The tree-sitters weren't going anywhere, however. They began installing a system of ropes and pulleys, allowing them to haul up food, water, sleeping bags, and the supplies they needed to build simple sleeping platforms. When their little houses in the trees were complete, they settled in and made themselves comfortable. They read books and played guitars, watched the birds, and listened to the night sounds of the forest.

Meanwhile, their protest was big the news in New Zealand, calling attention to the ongoing destruction of ancient woodlands. It caused such a stir that the government finally bowed to public pressure and stopped all future logging of native old-growth forests. Best of all, Pureora was turned into a national park.

Then, having achieved a stunning success, Stephen and his friends left the forest as peacefully as they'd come, and went home.

# FATHER LUIS OLIVARES AND THE SANCTUARY MOVEMENT

## *Doing unto Others*

Father Luis Olivares was an important man. As the treasurer of his religious order, he was in charge of its financial investments. So Wall Street bankers flew him to New York, put him up in expensive hotels, and took him by limousine to fancy restaurants. Having grown up poor, he loved feeling rich. He even dressed the part, wearing black silk suits and Gucci shoes.

Then he met the unforgettable César Chávez, the charismatic union leader who'd devoted his life to helping migrant farm workers. Comparing himself to this humble, almost saintly man, Father Luis was ashamed of the choices he'd made. The change of heart that followed was so radical and profound that he compared it to the conversion of St. Paul: one minute he was living the lush life in New York; the next, he was serving the poor as a parish priest in East Los Angeles. For the first time since taking holy orders, he truly felt he was doing God's work.

Five years later, in 1985, he would once again rethink his mission. In faraway Central America, brutal civil wars were raging in El Salvador and Guatemala, causing hundreds of thousands of terrified refugees to flee the violence of their ruined countries and head north in search of safety. But the U.S. government, for political reasons, treated Central Americans differently from other refugees. They were almost never granted asylum. Instead, they were sent home to face the vengeance of the death squads. Few who returned were likely to survive.

Since many of the refugees were in Los Angeles, Father Luis opened his doors to them, declaring his church a place of sanctuary. Some slept in the basement, others in the church hall, and when there was no room left, other churches and synagogues took them in. Parishioners brought them clothes and food, helped them find work, and enrolled their children in schools.

Father Luis didn't care that what they was doing was illegal, or that he'd angered both the immigration authorities and the archbishop of Los Angeles. He was obeying a higher law, the one that commanded him to be merciful, to care for the poor, feed the hungry, house the stranger, and clothe the naked. He was very clear about his mission now.

And he was not alone. The sanctuary movement spread all across the United States in the 1980s, with over five hundred congregations—Catholics, Jews, Lutherans, Presbyterians, Methodists, Baptists, Quakers, Mennonites, and many others—welcoming Central American refugees to sacred places of safety and saving many, many lives.

# TANK MAN

## *No One Ever Learned His Name*

In the spring and summer of 1989, a massive wave of protest rolled across China. From Mongolia in the north to Hong Kong in the south, people were out in the streets waving flags, carrying banners, and calling for change. They wanted democracy, the right to speak freely, and an end to forty years of repressive one-party rule. The government responded by declaring war on its citizens.

As many as three hundred thousand troops, along with tanks and armored personnel carriers, were sent to the capital to put the rebellion down. The standoff reached its climax on June 3 in what has come to be known as the "Beijing Massacre." By the time it was over, thousands had died, the army was in complete control, and still more tanks were rolling in to occupy and reinforce the city. It was then that something remarkable happened: a young man, neatly dressed in a white shirt and black pants, a leather satchel and a shopping bag in his hands, walked into the street and stood directly in the path of an advancing column of tanks. When the lead driver tried to go around him, the man skipped to the side and stopped, once again blocking the way. He shouted and waved his shopping bags. *Stop!* his gestures said. *Go away!*

The crowds lining the sidewalks and the press photographers out on the balconies of the Beijing Hotel, frantically shooting pictures and taking videos, were stunned by the man's incredible determination. Surely any moment he'd be killed. Yet he doggedly refused to give up.

Next, he climbed up onto the body of the tank and started banging on the turret, shouting at the soldiers inside. Two hatches opened, and heads appeared. After a brief exchange, the man climbed down and the tanks started moving. Once again he blocked their way.

Finally, two figures ran out, grabbed the man by his arms, and hurried him away—whether to help him or harm him, nobody knows. No one ever learned his name.

Tank Man's protest didn't bring change to China. But courage is contagious, and the stunning image of an ordinary man single-handedly facing down a column of tanks was broadcast all over the world. Far away, in Eastern Europe, pro-democracy activists looked at those photos and thought, *If he can stand up to power like that, then so can we.*

Five months later, on November 9, 1989, the Berlin Wall came down. Two years after that, the Soviet Union collapsed and the Cold War came to an end.

Tank Man, wherever you are, you made a difference.

# NELSON MANDELA

## *The Most Famous Prisoner in the World*

For nearly three hundred years, South Africa had been ruled by Dutch and British colonists. Though the population was overwhelmingly black, only whites could vote or hold office. And they governed the country under a system called *apartheid* in which the races were kept strictly apart. Nonwhites could work in the cities, cleaning houses or tending gardens, but they had to live elsewhere—in squalid black townships, many with no electricity, clean water, or schools for the children. And they were required to carry passbooks at all times, showing their racial designation and where they belonged. Naturally, the black majority hated these laws.

In 1943, a young law student named Nelson Mandela joined the African National Congress, a party that was working to bring an end to apartheid and gain voting rights for all. Mandela was a natural leader and quickly rose through the ranks, soon coming to the government's attention. Over the next twenty years, he would be frequently arrested or banned from speaking in public. Finally, in 1964, Mandela and seven others were charged with conspiring to overthrow the government and sentenced to life in the notorious Robben Island Prison.

Mandela would grow old there, spending his days at hard labor, living in a tiny concrete cell with a straw mat on the floor to sleep on. Yet he never stopped working, studying, and planning, as if he somehow knew his story wasn't yet over. When the moment came, he'd be ready.

Meanwhile, the apartheid system and the arrest of Mandela had made South Africa the "skunk of the world." Sports teams refused to play there, musicians wouldn't sing there, and the song "Free Nelson Mandela" became a Top Ten hit in Britain. The United Nations voted to ban the sale of weapons to South Africa. Britain and the U.S. imposed economic sanctions.

Finally, under intense international pressure, the government set Mandela free and ended the apartheid system. In an odd twist of fate, Mandela shared the 1993 Nobel Peace Prize with President F. W. de Klerk, the man who had released him from prison. The following year, with all citizens allowed to vote, Mandela was elected South Africa's first black president.

Mandela's dream was to make South Africa a "Rainbow Nation" in which all races could prosper. So he appointed whites as well as blacks to important government positions. Then he formed a Truth and Reconciliation Commission where victims could be heard and crimes confessed. Then, following Mandela's example, all was forgiven "for the sake of peace."

# School bars door to youth with AIDS

**By Christopher M. MacNeil**
Tribune staff writer

RUSSIAVILLE, Ind. — The mother of a local 13-year-old AIDS patient who has been barred from attending classes at Western Middle School today accused the school administration of "running around a problem they thought they wouldn't have to deal with."

Jeanne E. White, whose son, Ryan, was diagnosed with the usually fatal virus in December, said she thinks Western administrators "hoped Ryan would be sicker than he is now so that they wouldn't have to deal with him at school."

Tuesday, Western Superintendent James O. Smith announced that Ryan, an incoming seventh-grader, would not be allowed in school because he has acquired immune deficiency syndrome, the lethal virus that renders the body's disease-fighting ability powerless.

However, an interim set of guidelines released Tuesday by the state Board of Health recommended that school-age AIDS patients who feel well enough should be in school.

"But any person with AIDS is going to be sick an awful lot and there will be plenty of times when it might become a rather difficult administrative problem," said Dr. James Barrett, director of the state board's communicable disease division.

Meanwhile, the public nurse for the Howard County Board of Health this morning did not confirm nor deny a reported claim by Smith that his decision to ban Ryan from the classroom is backed by the health department.

"We did not receive the (state's) guidelines until yesterday (Tuesday). They're under advisement by us, and as such we can't make any further comment," said Nancy Mickelson.

She did say, however, that courses of action taken by corporations in dealing with AIDS children are "school decisions."

It was Ryan's case that prompted the state to prescribe the guidelines, according to a state health official.

Of the 45 confirmed AIDS patients statewide — three in Howard County — Ryan is believed to be the only one of school age.

Two other Howard County residents are among the 29 AIDS deaths in Indiana.

Ryan said this morning he feels "real fine" physically and stressed he is still passing his Kokomo Tribune paper route. He stressed even more he is "upset" with Smith's decision not to allow him in school.

"I want to go back," Ryan said.

Smith did not return any calls to the Tribune today. But he said in a published report that he based his decision on the "unknowns and uncertainties (about AIDS)" and "the inhertent fear that would generate among classmates.

"We are obligated to provide an education for the child," Smith added, explaining Ryan "will have to receive instruction at home."

# RYAN WHITE

*I Wasn't Welcome Anywhere*

His dreams were modest: he wanted to go to school, spend time with his friends, then graduate and go to college. But Ryan's life was complicated. He'd been born with hemophilia, a serious blood disorder. To prevent excessive bleeding, he was treated with a blood product called factor VIII, which provided the clotting protein his body lacked.

Then, in December of 1984, Ryan got very sick. It turned out that his factor VIII had been contaminated with a new virus known as HIV. Now Ryan had end-stage AIDS. He had just turned thirteen, and the doctors said he had maybe six months to live.

But to everyone's surprise, he got better. Soon he felt well enough to go back to school. His doctors said it was safe, that he wouldn't be a danger to his classmates. But people knew little about AIDS back then, just that it was deadly and there was no cure. Since they were terrified of the disease, they were also afraid of Ryan. His request was denied.

Ryan and his mother decided to fight the system. It became a year-long nightmare of petitions, appeals, and restraining orders, with lawyers, judges, and county health officials all weighing in on Ryan's future. And when he was finally allowed to go back to school, he was taunted by bullies and made to use a special bathroom and eat with disposable forks and spoons. Then a shot was fired through the family's living room window.

By then Ryan's case had made him famous. He was written about in newspapers and magazines. He spoke to the President's Commission on AIDS and appeared on national TV. At a time when more and more people were dying of AIDS, Ryan become the human face of a terrible new disease, informing and inspiring a nation, turning the tide against prejudice and fear.

Meanwhile, the Whites had moved to another town. But before Ryan arrived at his new school, the student body president, Jill Stuart, organized an information session, bringing in doctors to talk to the students and staff about AIDS. So Ryan was met with kindness when he got there. He made friends. He had a date for the prom. He did everything but go to college.

Shortly before his high school graduation, Ryan died, at the age of eighteen. More than 1,500 people came to his funeral. First Lady Barbara Bush was there. Elton John sang. And four months after that, Congress passed the Ryan White CARE Act in his honor, providing medical services for low-income or uninsured patients living with HIV/AIDS.

# AI WEIWEI

## *Remembering*

Ai Weiwei spent his childhood in labor camps in remote parts of northern China, far from their family home in Beijing. His father, a famous poet, had been sent there as punishment for criticizing the government. His job was cleaning the communal toilets. Ai concluded that words and ideas were powerful and dangerous things—for why else would they punish a man so harshly for simply writing what he believed?

In 1976, the family was allowed to return to Beijing. Ai was nineteen then, at a turning point in his life, and he decided to be an artist. After a few years of study in China, he moved to the United States, where he attended art schools, worked odd jobs, and painted lots of pictures nobody wanted to buy. Ai called himself an artist then, but deep down he knew it wasn't true. Finally, when he heard his father was ill, he went home.

After twelve years of living in the West, he'd forgotten what China was like, how you had to be careful because a person could be crushed for saying the wrong thing. Strangely, this was exactly what he'd needed as an artist—something to push back against, something daring and important to say. The more his art became a form of creative protest, the more meaningful it was.

In 2008, a massive earthquake shook Sichuan province. A shocking percentage of the victims were children whose schools had collapsed on top of them. The buildings should have been strong enough to withstand an earthquake, but the government had built them on the cheap. Now it was covering up the scandal, censoring news about the children's deaths.

So Ai went on his blog and recruited a hundred volunteers to go to Sichuan and visit the disaster zone. They went door-to-door, talking to thousands of heartbroken parents and collecting the names of every one of the 5,219 children who'd died. When Ai published the list on his blog, the government shut it down. So he took his protest to the world.

An exhibition of his art was already being planned by a museum in Munich, Germany. Now he added a powerful new work to honor the lost children of Sichuan. He chose a simple quote from one of the victims' mothers. Then he spelled it out in giant Chinese characters on an enormous banner that ran the entire length of the massive building. But it wasn't really a banner—it was a collage made from nine thousand children's backpacks. It read "She lived happily on this earth for seven years." He called the piece *Remembering*. No one who saw it could ever forget.

# "IT GETS BETTER" PROJECT

## *I Wish I Could Have Told Him*

On September 8, 2010, a fifteen-year-old boy named Billy Lucas came home from school and took his own life. For years he'd been tormented by bullies who said he was gay. That very afternoon, he'd been told he didn't deserve to live. It had been one taunt too many.

The news of Billy's death shocked the nation. Then the full scope of the problem was revealed as more names were added to the list of despairing teens who'd given up hope.

Dan Savage, an author and gay-rights activist, read Billy's story and remembered his own dreadful high school experience. "I wish I could have talked to this kid for five minutes," he wrote in one of his columns. "I wish I could have told him that, however bad things were, however isolated and alone he was, it gets better." Then it occurred to him that, while it was too late to save Billy and the others who'd followed, there were countless others, all over the world, who were going through the same thing. At least he could talk to *them*.

So he and his partner, Terry Miller, made a video and posted it online. They talked about the cruelty they'd endured at school, and how painful it had been. But they'd gotten through it, they said, and moved on to a life that was meaningful and full of joy. Anyone could tell, hearing their words and seeing them together, how much better things could get.

That video was the beginning of a remarkable internet-based nonprofit, the "It Gets Better" Project. Its mission is to "uplift, empower and connect LGBTQ+ youth around the globe." And it certainly succeeded. Thousands of videos started pouring in, from ordinary people as well as famous actors, singers, and politicians. Some were LGBTQ+, while others were straight. But they all had the same message: Hang in there. It gets better.

Barack Obama made a video. So did Justin Bieber, Neil Patrick Harris, Lady Gaga, Stephen Colbert, Katy Perry, Ellen DeGeneres, and Kermit the Frog. Group videos were posted by employees of Apple, Microsoft, Facebook, Adobe, and Pixar. Universities made group videos. So did churches, hospitals, and sports teams, from the Boston Red Sox to the LA Dodgers.

Today, because one man wished he could have saved one child, then came up with a brilliant idea that grew into a powerful movement for good, there are "It Gets Better" projects in countries all over the world—healing wounds and changing lives, one story at a time.

IT

GETS

BETTER!

# MARCH FOR OUR LIVES

## *Snowflakes*

On Valentine's Day, 2018, a troubled former student returned to Marjory Stoneman Douglas High School in Parkland, Florida, armed with an AR-15 semiautomatic rifle. Before the nightmare was over, seventeen students and staff members lay dead. Seventeen more were injured. The survivors were left with a mountain of grief—and a mountain of rage. Why did this keep happening? Why couldn't kids feel safe in their schools? Why was no one doing anything about it?

The next evening, following a candlelight vigil, three of the survivors—Cameron Kasky, Alex Wind, and Sofie Whitney—went to Cameron's house to talk. They felt very strongly that something needed to happen in response to the shooting: a powerful movement to prevent gun violence. But they'd have to work quickly, before the news cycle moved on to something else. They chose a name for their movement, "Never Again," and stayed up all night making plans.

Others soon joined the group, including David Hogg and Emma González. And within four days they had gone on Twitter to announce a demonstration, the March for Our Lives, to be held in Washington, D.C., on March 24.

The results exceeded their wildest hopes. Not only did hundreds of thousands travel to Washington for the protest, but millions gathered in eight hundred cities across the U.S.—and in thirty-two countries around the world—to march in solidarity with them.

That summer, the Parkland students embarked on a two-month cross-country bus tour, visiting seventy-five cities, holding rallies and giving speeches, calling for commonsense gun laws, and encouraging people to vote for change. The tour ended in Newtown, Connecticut, where five years before, another shooter had walked into Sandy Hook Elementary and killed twenty first-graders and six adults. The survivors of that horrific shooting, now in middle or high school, were inspired to start protests of their own.

Some critics made fun of the students by calling them "snowflakes"—fragile and weak and sure to melt away. David Hogg responded on Twitter. "What happens when all the snowflakes vote?" he wrote. "That's called an avalanche." And indeed, their efforts brought an avalanche of change. By the end of that year, sixty-nine separate gun-control measures had been passed by legislatures in more than half of the states in the union. And there's more to come.

# GRETA THUNBERG

## *Our House Is on Fire!*

On August 20, 2018, inspired by the Parkland students' March for Our Lives, a fifteen-year-old girl stood outside the Swedish parliament holding a homemade sign. It said *Skolstrejk för klimatet*—School Strike for the Climate. Her name was Greta Thunberg, she was fifteen years old, and she was about to start a global revolution.

She'd been eight when she first learned about global warming, and it had stunned her. She couldn't imagine why no one seemed upset about it. Why it wasn't front-page news. And why the governments of the world weren't doing everything possible to stop climate change before it was too late to save the planet. Couldn't they understand that this was a crisis?

Now, inspired by the activism of the Parkland students in America, Greta decided to go on strike to fight climate change. Every Friday she skipped school and stood with her sign outside the parliament building. Soon the media picked up her story. Pictures of Greta were all over the Internet. And in interviews, she astonished reporters with her passionate, articulate answers. Her words were so compelling that, three months after beginning her strike, she was asked to give a talk at TEDxStockholm. Next, she was invited to speak at the United Nations Climate Change Conference, followed by an appearance at the World Economic Forum.

"Our house is on fire!" she told them. "I want you to panic!"

In one speech, she pictured her seventy-fifth birthday, with imaginary grandchildren gathered around her. "Maybe they will ask me about you," she said, "the people who were around back in 2018. Maybe they will ask why you didn't do anything while there still was time to act."

As Greta and her cause became an international sensation, young people all over the world followed her lead. Soon a wave of student protests spread through Europe and crossed the Atlantic to Canada, the U.S., Mexico, and South America. It spread south into Africa and east to India and on to East Asia, then swept down under to Australia and New Zealand.

During the week of September 20–27, 2019, more than 7.6 million people from 185 countries joined Greta in what has been called the greatest climate protest in history. Someday, perhaps on their seventy-fifth birthdays, those students may join her in telling their grandchildren that when the crisis came, they took a stand. And perhaps it will have made all the difference.

## ADDITIONAL INFORMATION

### TAKE A STAND

Several of the stories in this book are about young people taking a stand—Claudette Colvin, the Greensboro Four, the children who marched in Birmingham, Ryan White and Jill Stuart, the Marjory Stoneman Douglas students, and Greta Thunberg. And of course there there are many others, from Malala Yousufzai, whose courageous fight for girls' education earned her a Nobel Prize, to the countless students, over the years and across the globe, who have protested wars and fought injustice.

So you may be wondering if you, too, could make a difference. The answer is yes. Whatever you're concerned about—whether it's homelessness, intolerance, bullying, climate change, or something really small and local that is hurting someone else—reach out to those with the power to make big changes. Then ask yourself what part you can play. Be creative.

Melati and Isabel Wijsen, sisters living on the Indonesian Island of Bali, were only ten and twelve years old when they asked themselves that question. They were concerned about the masses of plastic trash that was covering Bali's beaches, flowing down its waterways into the ocean, turning their beautiful home into a polluted "island of garbage."

One night they sat on the couch and had a brainstorming session. Then they gathered a team of kids who wanted to help. They chose a motto ("Bye Bye Plastic Bags"), designed a logo, and printed them on T-shirts and stickers. They wore the T-shirts and gave away the stickers to any stores that agreed to stop handing out plastic bags. They built a website. They organized clean-up-the-beach days. And they collected signatures on a petition, which they sent to the governor.

In 2019, six years after the two little girls started their campaign to clean up the island, Bali officially banned single-use plastic—from Styrofoam boxes and drinking straws to that greatest offender, plastic bags. Today, their movement has teams in more than twenty-five locations world-wide and is growing. Maybe there's one near you.

But if you dream of making positive change in the world, don't let anyone discourage you by saying you're too young. "We're not telling you it's going to be easy," Isabel said. "We're telling you it's going to be worth it."

### MORE ABOUT NONVIOLENT RESISTERS

#### Harriet Tubman
Petry, Ann. *Harriet Tubman: Conductor on the Underground Railroad*. New York: Amistad, 2018.
Cline-Ransome, Lesa, and James E. Ransome. *Before She Was Harriet*. New York: Holiday House, 2017.
Weatherford, Carole Boston and Kadir Nelson. *Moses: When Harriet Tubman Led Her People to Freedom*. New York: Hyperion, 2006.

#### Elizabeth Cady Stanton
Zimet, Susan, and Tod Hasak-Lowy. *Roses and Radicals: The Epic Story of How American Women Won the Right to Vote*. New York: Viking: 2018.

#### Woody Guthrie
Partridge, Elizabeth. *This Land Was Made for You and Me: The Life and Songs of Woody Guthrie*. New York: Viking, 2002.
woodyguthrie.org/

#### Mohandas Gandhi
Miller, Derek. *Mahatma Gandhi: March to Independence (Peaceful Protestors)*. New York: Cavendish Square Publishing, 2018.
DW Documentary. "Mahatma Gandhi—Dying for Freedom." YouTube video. https://www.youtube.com/watch?v=hpZwCRInrgo

#### Irena Sendler
Rubin, Susan Goldman, and Bill Farnsworth. *Irena Sendler and the Children of the Warsaw*. New York: Holiday House, 2011.
Jewish Virtual Library. "Irena Sendler (1910–2008)." https://www.jewishvirtuallibrary.org/irena-sendler

#### The Hollywood Ten
"The Hollywood Blacklist: 1947–1960." YouTube video. https://www.youtube.com/watch?v=nJzV6-wJ3SQ

#### Claudette Colvin and Rosa Parks
Parks, Rosa, and Jim Haskins. *Rosa Parks: My Story*. New York: Puffin Books, 1999.
Hoose, Phillip. *Claudette Colvin: Twice Toward Justice*. New York: Farrar, Straus and Giroux, 2009.
Giovanni, Nikki, and Bryan Collier. *Rosa*. New York: Square Fish, 2007.

#### Ruth Bader Ginsburg
Carmon, Irin, and Shana Knizhnik. *Notorious RBG Young Readers' Edition: The Life and Times of Ruth Bader Ginsburg*. New York: Harper Collins, 2017.
Levy, Debbie, and Elizabeth Baddely. *I Dissent: Ruth Bader Ginsburg Makes Her Mark*. New York: Simon & Schuster, 2016.
Winter, Jonah, and Stacy Innerst. *Ruth Bader Ginsburg: The Case of R.B.G. vs. Inequality*. New York: Harry N. Abrams, 2017.

#### The Greensboro Lunch Counter Sit-in
Pinkney, Andrea Davis, and Brian Pinkney. *Sit-In: How Four Friends Stood Up by Sitting Down*. New York: Little, Brown Books for Young Readers, 2010.
"Reflections on the Greensboro Lunch Counter." YouTube video. https://www.youtube.com/watch?v=uFQ3ZCAgAA0

#### Martin Luther King Jr.
"Letter From Birmingham Jail." YouTube video. https://www.youtube.com/watch?v=XIpfCVt2eb4
Lewis, John, Andrew Aydin, and Nate Powell. *March Book One*. Marietta, GA: Top Shelf Productions, 2013.
Rappaport, Doreen, and Bryan Collier. *Martin's Big Words: The Life of Dr. Martin Luther King, Jr.* New York: Hyperion, 2007.

#### Larry Itliong, Dolores Huerta, and César Chávez
Brimner, Larry Dane. *Strike!: The Farm Workers' Fight for Their Rights*. Honesdale, PA: Calkins Creek, 2014.
Brown, Monica, and Joe Cepeda. *Side by Side/Lado a Lado: The Story of Dolores Huerta and Cesar Chavez/La Historia de Dolores Huerta y César Chávez*. New York: HarperCollins Español, 2010.

#### Richard Oakes and the Occupation of Alcatraz
The Two-Way, an NPR blog. "Richard Oakes, Who Occupied Alcatraz For Native Rights, Gets A Birthday Honor." https://www.npr.org/sections/thetwo-way/2017/05/22/529504340/richard-oakes-who-occupied-alcatraz-for-native-rights-gets-a-birthday-honor

#### The Tree-Sitters of Pureora
https://en.wikipedia.org/wiki/Pureora_Forest_Park

#### Father Luis Olivares and the Sanctuary Movement
http://amigos805.com/professor-mario-garcias-biography-of-father-luis-olivares-illuminates-the-birth-of-the-sanctuary-movement-in-los-angeles/

#### Tank Man
Mara, Wil. *Tiananmen Square Massacre in China (Cornerstones of Freedom: Third Series)*. New York: Children's Press, 2013.
"Tank Man." YouTube video. https://www.youtube.com/watch?v=qq8zFLIftGk

#### Nelson Mandela
The Nelson Mandela Foundation, and Umlando Wezithombe. *Nelson Mandela: The Authorized Comic Book*. New York: W.W. Norton, 2009.
Keller, Bill. *Tree Shaker: The Life of Nelson Mandela*. New York: Kingfisher, 2013.
Nelson, Kadir. *Nelson Mandela*. New York: Katherine Tegen Books, 2013.

#### Ryan White
"The Right to Live a Normal Life: Ryan White's Story." Vimeo video. https://vimeo.com/118844741

#### Ai Weiwei
Weiwei, Ai. "Ai Weiwei: The artwork that made me the most dangerous person in China." *The Guardian*, February 15, 2018. https://www.theguardian.com/artanddesign/2018/feb/15/ai-weiwei-remembering-sichuan-earthquake

#### "It Gets Better" Project
https://itgetsbetter.org/

#### March for Our Lives
The March for Our Lives Founders. *Glimmer of Hope: How Tragedy Sparked a Movement*. New York: Razorbill, 2018.
https://marchforourlives.org/

#### Greta Thunberg
Thunberg, Greta. *No One Is Too Small to Make a Difference*. New York: Penguin, 2019.
Greta's Fridays for Future webpage: https://www.fridaysforfuture.org/
https://www.youtube.com/watch?v=ns54HAZgHvY
Follow Greta on X and Instagram at @GretaThunberg.